BECAUSE
HE
LIVES

*The Hope, Promise, & Truth
of the Resurrection*

From the writings of

Sandy Adams
Jon Courson
Damian Kyle
Bill Stonebraker

Copyright © 2004 by Damian Kyle
Published by Calvary Chapel Publishing (CCP), a resource ministry of
Calvary Chapel of Costa Mesa.
3800 South Fairview Road
Santa Ana, CA 92704
Scripture taken from the New King James Version.
Copyright © 1982 by Thomas Nelson, Inc. Used by permission. All rights
reserved.

Copyright © 2004 by Sandy Adams
Published by Chapter By Chapter Books
Calvary Chapel Stone Mountain
1969 McDaniels Bridge Road, Lilbum, GA 30047
(770) 736-2828
email: ccsm@ mindspring.com
www.calvarychapel.com/lilbum
Scripture taken from the New King James Version of the Bible.
Copyright © 1982 by Thomas Nelson, Inc. Used by permission. All rights
reserved.

Copyright © 2004 by Jon Courson
Published by Applegate Christian Fellowship
Jacksonville, Oregon 97530
All Scripture taken from the King James Version of the Bible.

Copyright © 2004 by Bill Stonebraker
Published by Calvary Chapel Honolulu
1190 Nuuanu Avenue, Honolulu, HI 96817
www.calvarychapel.org/honolulu
Scripture taken from the NEW AMERICAN STANDARD BIBLE®,
© Copyright The Lockman Foundation 1960,1963,1968,1971, 1972,
1973,1975,1977,1995 Used by permission.

ISBN 0-9676661-8-X

All rights reserved. No part of this publication may be reproduced, stored
in a retrieval system, or transmitted in any form by any means, electronic,
mechanical, photocopy, recording, or otherwise, without the prior permission
of the publisher, except as provided by USA copyright law.

Printed in the United States of America

Contents

"ACCESS"
by Damian Kyle

*The soldiers came and broke the legs of the first
and of the other who was crucified with Him.
But when they came to Jesus and saw that He
was already dead, they did not break His legs.
But one of the soldiers pierced His side with a
spear, and immediately blood and water came
out. ... For these things were done that the
Scripture should be fulfilled, "Not one of His
bones shall be broken." ... And "They shall look
on Him whom they pierced."*

—John 19:32–37

In this passage, God, by His Holy Spirit, paints
a striking picture of Jesus on the cross: Jesus' head
is laid down, He has dismissed His Spirit, and that
glorious, incomparable body is now lifeless. The eyes
of Jesus are now closed. The hands that had healed
the sick, cleansed the lepers, blessed the children,
and multiplied the loaves and fish are now pierced
by six-inch iron nails, covered with blood, and hang
completely limp.

As we consider this scene, we have the ultimate representation of the wickedness of the human heart—the wickedness of my heart. We have a picture of the seriousness of sin, not only the general sin of the whole world, but the seriousness of even one, single sin.

The events that took place at Calvary and in the Temple as Jesus dismissed His Spirit radiate with God-ordained significance, meant to shout through the ages the implications of that death for all of mankind.

Justification Given

Imagine the scene. The Roman soldiers come to Jesus and recognize that He is already dead so they don't break His legs. But one of the soldiers does something interesting. He takes his spear, and with the efficiency of a man trained in war, thrusts it up under the ribcage of Jesus, into the thoracic cavity, and pierces the heart of Jesus. As quickly as he pulls the spear out of Jesus' side, a stream of blood and water flows behind it.

I think the water and the blood reveal that Jesus died with a broken heart. Notice I said that He died with a broken heart, not that He died of a broken heart. In the last couple hundred years, as physicians' understanding of the physiology of the human body has increased, they have looked at this scene and said that Jesus died of a broken heart. They draw this conclusion because it would seem that somehow Jesus' heart had ruptured. Somehow it had burst and had begun to leak blood into the water-like fluid of the pericardium, which is the sac that surrounds the heart. Thus when His pericardium and heart were pierced by the spear, out came both blood and water.

But we know from the Scriptures that Jesus didn't die of anything physical. He died when He dismissed His spirit to the Father (John 19:30). So it would be incorrect to say that He died of a broken heart, but it would be both correct and Scriptural to say He died with a broken heart.

When I trusted in the Lord Jesus for the forgiveness of my sins, the Bible teaches that I was justified by my faith in the Lord Jesus. A man or a woman is justified before God only on the basis of faith in the Lord Jesus. There isn't a justification by my faith and my works, much less justification before God on the basis of my works alone.

Justification is one of those terms that can be difficult to grasp. It means being declared righteous in the sight of God, being declared perfectly holy and right in the eyes of the Lord. A great definition for the word justified is, "just as if I'd never sinned." That's how God sees me, not because I never did sin, and not because

I don't fall short daily, but because when He looks at me, He sees the sacrifice of His Son. He sees His Son's blood. As a Christian, I am now in Christ Jesus.

Paul wrote in Romans 5:8, 9, "But God demonstrates His own love towards us, in that while we were still sinners, Christ died for us. Much more then, having now been justified by His blood, we shall be saved from wrath through Him." When I became a believer in the Lord Jesus, something wonderful happened in the accounting office in heaven—they pulled out the Damian Kyle file, which held a running record of all my sins. They had to truck it in because one guy couldn't carry it over. All of the failure, all of the wickedness, every thought, every action, everything I should have done, but didn't do—all of it was recorded in that file. When I trusted in the Lord Jesus for my salvation, God called for that file, took it, and separated it from me as far as the east is from the west (Psalm 103:12). I'll never come into contact with it. I'll never be judged or incur God's wrath for a single thing that was contained within that file.

But He doesn't stop there. He then takes out this beautiful, clean white sheet of paper, stamps on it "righteous," and puts it in my file. The Bible says that when I trust in the Lord Jesus, His perfect righteousness is put to my account. So if you went to heaven and looked at the Damian Kyle file, that's what you'd find—a single sheet of paper in there with the word righteous stamped on it.

I'm thankful for what the blood of Christ has meant to my past and for the forgiveness of my sin. But you know, when I came to the Lord, I didn't want to enter into the Christian life just being forgiven and then continue living the same, stinking, dirty, filthy, defiling life that I was living. I needed to be changed from what I was. I needed a practical cleansing in my life. Just as water cleanses us physically, I needed cleansing with a different kind of water to purify me spiritually from what I still was. When I came to know the Lord, my greatest concern was not escaping hell. I needed someone to save me from me and from the wickedness and dominion of my sin and my flesh. I needed that cleansing.

As we think about the water that came from Jesus' side, I am reminded of what the Apostle Paul wrote in Ephesians 5:25, 26, "Christ also loved the church and gave Himself for her, that He might sanctify and cleanse her with the washing of water by the word." Here Paul describes that beautiful, daily, active cleansing work of Jesus in my life. It comes through reading and meditating on His Word. Jesus told His disciples, "You are already clean because of the word which I have spoken to you" (John 15:3). The psalmist wrote in Psalm 119, "How can a young man cleanse his way? By taking heed according to Your word" (v. 9). So that practical cleansing takes place because of the relationship that I have with Him through His death upon the cross for me, but it takes place as I spend time with Him in His Word.

One of fascinating things about the blood and water coming out of Jesus' side is that so much of the ministry of the Old Testament priests dealt with those same two fluids. Under the Old Covenant, there was constant repetition concerning the blood and the water, as the priests would offer the sacrifices for their own sins and for the sins of the people.

The writer of the book of Hebrews understood the importance of the blood and water. In chapter 10, verse 19, he said, "Therefore, brethren, having boldness to enter the Holiest by the blood of Jesus, by a new and living way which He consecrated for us, through the veil, that is, His flesh, and having a High Priest over the house of God, let us draw near with a true heart in full assurance of faith. ..." And then notice this: he says, "... having our hearts sprinkled from an evil conscience and our bodies washed with pure water." The Lord Jesus is both the forgiver and the sanctifier in our lives.

Now let me take you back to the iron mallet used to break the dying men's legs and the soldier's spear that was thrust into Jesus' side. Notice in verse 36 John writes, "For these things were done that the Scripture should be fulfilled." All that happened to Jesus was in fulfillment of the Scriptures. So once again, watch the Roman soldiers as they raise the mallet and lower it on the feet and on the legs of those two thieves. (The legs and feet of the prisoners were crushed so that they could no longer support the weight of their bodies, thereby hastening death by suffocation.) Watch them come to Jesus, find Him dead, and put the mallet down—they don't crush His feet; they don't crush His ankles; they don't crush His legs. But instead, watch this one soldier plunge his spear up under the ribcage of Jesus, piercing His side.

Watch it from the Apostle John's vantage point. As he's witnessing the scene, two great Old Testament prophecies are filling his mind. The first is from Exodus 12. It stated that the Passover Lamb could not have one of his bones broken (v. 46). So if Jesus had had a single one of His bones broken at any point throughout the progression of the crucifixion, then He could not be the Messiah as prescribed by the Scriptures. John knew that. Imagine what he was feeling as he watched the mallet approach Jesus.

The second prophecy is from Zechariah 12. Concerning the Messiah, Zechariah said that the day would come when they would look on Him whom they had pierced, and mourn for Him as one mourns for an only son, and grieve for Him as one grieves for a firstborn (v. 10). Well, you can only look upon one who has been pierced if the piercing has occurred. As John looks at Jesus and hears Him cry, "It is finished," and as Jesus gives up His spirit and dies without any piercing, John must be wondering: How can He be the Messiah according to Zechariah 12? Why would anyone pierce Him now that He's dead? Imagine the emptiness he must have felt as he remembered that prophecy and considered the improbability of its fulfillment through Jesus in light of those circumstances.

These two prophets, Moses and Zechariah, come together declaring that the Messiah would die, and that in His death, not a single one of His bones would be broken and yet His side would be pierced. How in the world can those two prophecies come together? John is pondering these things because it doesn't seem to him that they can be fulfilled. That's the beauty of it. It doesn't make any sense. If they were cruel enough to thrust Him through His heart while He was dead, why not cruel enough to crush His legs at the same time? And if they were sympathetic enough not to crush His legs, then why bother to pierce Him?

Yet, as we observe the scene that John was watching with those verses in mind, and we follow those Roman soldiers, as illogical as it is, they do exactly what the prophets said they would do hundreds and thousands of years before Jesus was ever born. Why? Because He is the Messiah. Because He is the Passover Lamb, come not to redeem man from the bondage of Egypt, as cruel and as harsh as that bondage was, but come to redeem man from a greater bondage—the bondage of sin. How tragic that all of those religious leaders were now scurrying around the Temple, preparing for the Passover, when there, just a few hundred yards away, hanging lifeless on the cross, was the true Passover Lamb. God's Passover Lamb had already been offered. Just as God's judgment had passed over every home in Egypt that had blood applied to the doorposts and lintel of the home, so too God's judgment passes over us when He sees Jesus' blood applied to our lives by faith.

Paul wrote to the Corinthians, "For indeed Christ, our Passover, was sacrificed for us"—the Lamb who takes away the sin of the world (1 Corinthians 5: 7). But not only the sin of the world in a general sense, He is also the Lamb who will take away your sin. And just to be sure that the religious establishment in Jerusalem understood that Jesus is the ultimate sacrifice for sin, God made it undeniably clear through an act designed to speak volumes to them.

Access Granted

Now when the sixth hour had come, there was darkness over the whole land until the ninth hour. And at the ninth hour Jesus cried out with a loud voice, saying, "Eloi, Eloi, lama sabachthani?" which is translated, "My God, My God, why have You forsaken Me?" And Jesus cried out with a loud voice, and breathed His last. Then the veil of the temple was torn in two from top to bottom.

—Mark 15:33, 34, 37, 38

The second event proclaiming the message that Jesus is God's Son took place within the Temple just after Jesus' death. The Father chose that precise moment in time to do something absolutely staggering. He had been watching every move of Jesus upon the cross. He had been watching every move of mankind around Him. He'd been listening to all the mocking, all the blasphemy. He had heard every word that His Son cried out from the cross. Then when His Son uttered that final cry, laid down His head, and dismissed His spirit, the Father reached into the deepest part of the Temple, only a few hundred yards away from where Jesus was crucified, and tore the veil from top to bottom.

What was the veil? It was essentially a gigantic curtain. In the Temple built by Herod and used by the Jews, the veil was said to have been sixty feet high, thirty feet wide, and as thick as the breadth of a man's hand.

The veil separated two specific sections of the inner part of the Temple. The innermost part was called the Holy of Holies, the Most Holy Place, or the Holiest of All because God's very presence dwelled there. It was the place where He chose to meet with man. Outside of this cubicle-sized room was the Holy Place. There was an opening between the rooms, and the only barrier between them was the veil.

Now the interesting thing about the Temple is that it was, in a sense, a series of obstructions keeping man from reaching the Holy of Holies. In order to make your way from the outside city of Jerusalem into the innermost parts of the Temple, one had to move progressively through a series of courts, then through the Holy Place, in order to reach the Most Holy Place.

Not everyone could get there. If you were a

Gentile, that is a non-Jew, you would make your way to the Temple mount, and come to what is known as the court of the Gentiles. Eventually, you would come to a wall with an opening that had these words posted above it: "No Gentiles beyond this point under the price of death." As a Gentile, you couldn't ever go beyond that court.

If you were a female Jew, you could make your way through the court of the Gentiles into the court of the women, but no further. If you were a Jewish man, however, you could make your way through the court of the Gentiles, through the court of the women, and then into the court of the men, but you couldn't go into the Holy Place because that was reserved for the Levites. You could be a great and godly Jew from a tribe other than the tribe of Levi, and in your lifetime you would never enter into that room—never have access to it. But even if you were a Levite, you wouldn't be able to enter the Holy of Holies because only one man, the high priest, could go into the Holy of Holies, and he could only do so one day a year—on the Day of Atonement—and only after he had offered a sacrifice for his own sins and for the sins of the people.

Only one man, the high priest, could enter the presence of God one day out of the year, and only after he had offered sacrifices. For the other 364 days of the year, the darkness and the quiet in the Holy of Holies remained completely undisturbed. No one ever went in or came out.

The interesting thing about a veil is that it is essentially an instrument for concealing. It's something to hide behind. In regions of the world where women wear veils, it's to hide their faces. That's very much what this was. Everything about the Temple was a reminder to man of the fact that our sin has separated us from the one thing that we have been created for—a relationship with God.

Now God, following the death of His Son, reached down into the Temple, into the Holy of Holies itself, and tore the veil in two, creating an impact that would have been astounding for any Jewish person of that day.

I'm a Gentile—half Scottish and half Irish. I don't descend from a Jewish lineage. The same is true for a lot of us. We come from purely Gentile, pagan backgrounds, and all we've known is immediate access to God since we heard the Gospel. But the Jews, after having gone through the sacrificial system year in and year out, must have been astonished by the fact that God would tear that veil in two.

He made His presence known to the religious community in Jerusalem through the tearing of the veil. Darkness enveloped Calvary and the city of Jerusalem for three hours—that was for the common person. But early that morning the religious leaders had given Jesus up for crucifixion apart from any valid or lawful reasoning, and then escaped back to their Temple, concerned only with the business of getting ready for Passover and the other religious activities. They had escaped the darkness at the scene of the crucifixion and God's identification that this was His Son on the cross. And so He reserved a sign for the priests.

He tore the veil at 3:00 pm. This is fascinating because Jesus was crucified at the time of the Feast of Passover, and the Temple would have been a flurry of activity as the sacrifices were being prepared. It is highly probable that because it was a high holy day, Caiaphas, the high priest, was in that Holy Place, standing before the Holy of Holies. He was probably in the very act of offering incense on the altar that stood before the veil at the exact moment it was torn in two.

This same Caiaphas had tried Jesus earlier that morning in a trial that was nothing more than a sham, with groups of men bringing false accusations against Jesus. They couldn't get their stories to align, and eventually, in this religious environment, before an assembly of some portion of the Sanhedrin, it became so embarrassing to Caiaphas that he abandoned the entire plan. Finally, turning to Jesus Himself, he says, "I adjure you by the living God that You tell us if You are the Christ, the Son of God." Now here was an accusation that Jesus could respond to! So Jesus looked at Caiaphas and said, "It is as you have said. Nevertheless, I say to you, hereafter you will see the Son of Man sitting at the right hand of the Power, and coming on the clouds of heaven." When Caiaphas heard that, he tore his clothes and proclaimed to the religious rulers, "He has spoken blasphemy! What further need do we have of witnesses? Look, now you have heard His blasphemy." He asked the religious leaders, "Now what do you think?" And they answered, "He is deserving of death." Then they began to spit in Jesus' face and to beat Him and strike Him with the palms of their hands saying, "Prophesy to us, Christ, who is it that is hitting You now?" (See Matthew 26.)

Imagine Caiaphas standing before the veil, hearing that massive fabric tear. A sheet tearing can be heard for some distance. But hearing something that's four to six inches thick begin to tear is going to get your attention. And when God had finished tearing it from the top to the bottom, Caiaphas would be staring straight into the Holy of Holies. He had a problem because it wasn't the Day of Atonement. He had to be wondering if God was going to kill him right there on the spot.

I wonder if Caiaphas understood that God was communicating His complete rejection of him and all that he stood for. It's almost as if, when religious man would not be shocked at the murder of their Lord, God's Son, the Temple tore her garments like one who had been smitten with the deepest pain and shock imaginable. Every square inch of that Temple spoke of Jesus, and they missed it entirely.

Again, the tearing of the veil would have been astounding beyond description to the Jewish mind because in the Holy of Holies, nothing was to be moved, touched, or seen. And now Caiaphas is looking at the torn veil, hanging there awkwardly off of the hooks of gold and clasps of silver. It's drooped and lying to both sides, exposing the Holy of Holies to anyone who would care to look. God was communicating something else to Caiaphas. And He was (and is) communicating something to us, something wonderful, something astounding—the Old Covenant had been completely fulfilled. God was unveiling a New Covenant based on the sacrifice and shed blood of His Son. The old was giving way to the new, and so He tears the veil in half. He has provided a new Veil on the cross.

The writer of the book of Hebrews refers to Jesus as the Veil. No longer would the high priest pass through a fabric veil into the Holy of Holies for an intimate relationship with God. That had been replaced by a living Veil—the life and the body of the Lord Jesus. Now access to an intimate relationship with God is no longer limited to one man on one day of the year going through a physical veil. Now it's open to all of mankind any time they want through the Veil that had been provided on the cross. The way to immediate intimacy and relationship with God is through the Veil, through the body, through the Son, and through the blood.

So the veil in the Temple separating man from God had been replaced by a far greater Veil. And the old high priest gave way to a new High Priest, the Lord Jesus, who never fails, never sins, never has to offer a sacrifice for His sin. The old sacrifices that had been offered annually, even daily, were fulfilled in the Lord Jesus. The sacrifice of Calvary not only covers sin, but washes away sin once and for all. So now this New Covenant, this new agreement, this new relationship with God is based upon the blood of Jesus—His life, His sacrifice.

I suppose that if there were one word that I would write about that torn veil, it would be the word access.

What God was communicating in the tearing of that veil is that the way to God is now wide open to every single person. Everyone is welcome—Jew and Gentile alike. Everyone has full access to God.

Paul wrote to the Romans on this theme of access, "Therefore, having been justified by faith, we have peace with God through our Lord Jesus Christ, through whom also we have access by faith into this grace in which we stand, and rejoice in hope of the glory of God" (5:1, 2).

Similarly, he wrote to the Gentile believers in Ephesus, saying, in effect, "But now in Christ Jesus, you who were once afar off, you who would never have made it past the court of the Gentiles, you who would have been killed in the court of the women if you'd have tried to get any closer, you've been given access." Most of us, as Gentiles, have to work at understanding these things. The Jews understood it. Paul said, "Now in Christ Jesus you who once were far off have been brought near by the blood of Christ. For He Himself is our peace, who has made both one, and has broken down the middle wall of separation [that is, Jew and Gentile], having abolished in His flesh the enmity, that is, the law of commandments contained in ordinances, so as to create in Himself one new man from the two, thus making peace, and that He might reconcile them both to God in one body through the cross, thereby putting to death the enmity. And He came and preached peace to you who were afar off and to those who were near. For through Him we both have access to one Spirit to the Father" (Ephesians 2:13–18).

Writing again to the Ephesians, he said, "To me, who am less than the least of all the saints, this grace was given that I should preach among the Gentiles the unsearchable riches of Christ, and to make all see what is the fellowship of the mystery, which from the beginning of the ages has been hidden in God who created all things through Jesus Christ," and again, "In whom we have boldness and access with confidence through faith in Him" (Ephesians 3:8, 9, 12).

The Father has communicated to us through this torn veil that we can come to Him, and the reason we can come to Him is because He has invited us. He tore the veil. He provided the new Veil. Referring again to Hebrews 10, we are told that the veil represented the Body of Jesus. Because of Jesus' sacrifice, we have boldness to enter the Holy of Holies by a new and living way, which He consecrated for us through the Veil, that is, His flesh. Not a series of courts, rooms, and veils, but now only one Veil between God and man, now only one curtain to go through, only one life—the life of the Lord Jesus. I can have a personal relationship of my own! All of this helps us to understand what a privilege it is to go straight through Jesus. Because of His sacrifice, any believer can enter at any time into God's presence in prayer, praise, and thanksgiving.

The writer of the book of Hebrews put it this way, in light of what Jesus has done for us, "Let us therefore come boldly to the throne of grace, that we may obtain mercy and find grace to help in time of need" (4:16). What a staggering privilege to come before God boldly at His invitation, and then to receive mercy and grace when we do come boldly. Amazing!

God was communicating, in that torn veil, the essence of what Christianity is—a personal relationship with God. My own personal relationship with God, not a personal relationship with God through Calvary Chapel, the Roman Catholic Church, through a series of leaders, or your mom and dad. God wants a personal relationship with you, and He's paid a tremendous price for you to have that. He paid the price because He longs for it. And He knows that you need it. We are granted immediate access into the Holy of Holies because of His work and not ours.

Notice finally that He tore the veil from the top to the bottom, not from the bottom to the top. Why is this important? So we would know that salvation has come from heaven to man. It came from the top to the bottom. God is communicating not only access through that torn veil, but that the means of the access is now by grace, not by works. Not by tearing from the bottom up, my works reaching up to God, but God reaching down to me in grace so that I would never come to God based upon my works or my deeds, so that I would never not come to God because of my failure.

Do you ever fail? Do you ever sin? We all do. When I sin, I know I ought to go back to God right away, but I want to do a few good deeds first. So I start doing nice things, being really good for a day or two, and then I feel I can go to God. What have I done? I've tried to sew up the veil! I've sewn it with my own efforts. When He tore the veil, He didn't stop halfway and say, "Now it's going to take a little effort, but it's possible. You've got to climb up over the section that's not torn." When He tore that veil, there wasn't a single thread left joining the two halves, and what God was saying is that access isn't through Jesus plus even the smallest work of our own, not even the cutting of one thread. We can't add to it. Written above that Temple scene is the beautiful word access—no mediators, no gurus, no anything, just the Lord Jesus and a relationship with the Father through Him. It's an awesome thing to have the relationship that we have, to have the access that we have. The veil is rent; it's torn so that we can experience unlimited fellowship with Him all day, every day!

What a tremendous price the Father paid for us! The death of Jesus provides direct access to the Father, and the blood and water that flowed from His side represent His provision for our cleansing and forgiveness so we can each take full advantage of it. What a tragedy it would be to neglect so great a salvation. Won't you enter into the abundant life? God stands ready to receive you through the Veil— Jesus Christ.

Next, Pastor Sandy Adams considers the ramifications of the resurrection for our lives today.

Was the Ressurrection a Real Event?

EVIDENCE FOR THE RESURRECTION
By Sandy Adams

And if Christ is not risen, then our preaching is empty and your faith is also empty. Yes, and we are found false witnesses of God, because we have testified of God that He raised up Christ, whom He did not raise up—if in fact the dead do not rise. For if the dead do not rise, then Christ is not risen. And if Christ is not risen, your faith is futile; you are still in your sins!

—1 Corinthians 15:14-17

Pretend you pick up a newspaper and found the following report...

DATELINE JERUSALEM: In the aftermath of the annual celebration of the Resurrection of Jesus of Nazareth, this city was shocked by the announcement that a decomposed body, identified as that of Jesus, was found in a long-neglected tomb. Rumors circutated last week that a very important discovery was about to be announced.

Initial reaction of Christians here and around the world has been one of astonishment and bewilderment. We will have to wait and see just what the affect this discovery will have on the 2,000 year-old religion. But it appears that Christianity can no longer claim that, unlike other religions, the tomb of its founder is empty. A 2,000 year-old lie has come to an end.

Obviously this is a fictitious story, but what if this report proved reliable? Suddenly, in an instant, our faith would be come futile. All that we believe in and have staked our lives upon would collapse. Christianity is an empty religion without an empty tomb. It's the Resurrection of Christ that makes Christianity worthy of belief—the only option for the objective mind.

Over the centuries, countless religious leaders have promised their disciples eternal life. Scores of philosophers have provided ethical teachings to their followers. And religions galore promote subjective experiances among their adherents. Metaphysical goose bumps are as common as sliced bread. Likewise, Jesus promises eternal life, provides moral guidance, and produces spiritual experience, but here's the difference: Jesus went significantly, decisively, uniquely farther than anyone else has ever gone. Jesus didn't just expect us to take Him at His Word; He dared to base His promises and teachings on historically verifiable facts.

Christianity is what the historians call "falsifiable"—it can be proven or refuted; it's subject to the scrutiny and investigation of inquiring minds. Jesus did everything He taught His disciples and claimed about Himself to an objective, historical event that occurred in time and space, His Resurrection.

In the Gospels, Jesus told His disciples more than once that He was going to Jerusalem to be killed but that on the third day He would rise again. His identity, the credibility of His teaching, His ability to forgive sin and send the Holy Spirit, and His promise of eternal life all hinged on the Resurrection.

If death had held Him in its clutches. His whole life and ministry would have become suspect. If Jesus had gone the way of other men. He would have been branded a liar. Defeated and humiliated, He would have drifted into obscurity and become just another Israeli imposter, a forgotten, false messiah.

When news broke concerning the Resurrection, not every one was convinced. Following the Resurrection, the Apostle Paul stood before King Agrippa to give an account of his conversion. When his sanity was questioned by Festus, who was also in attendance, Paul gave this defense: "For the king, before whom I also speak freely, knows these things; for I am convinced that none of these things escapes his attention, since this thing was not done in a corner." The implication is that if the king had been out of his house at all—to the Temple or the market—he would have known about the Resurrection. The news was all over town. The stone was rolled away not to let Jesus out, but to let us look in and see the empty tomb for ourselves. Jesus Christ is alive. Paul challenged Agrippa to examine the evidence, to investigate.

Could Paul's case for the Resurrection stand up in today's courtroom under the pressure of cross-examination? Could it survive the scrutiny of the skeptic? I'm convinced it can. The weight of the evidence is actually overwhelming.

Two pieces of principle evidence support the case. We'll call them exhibit A and B. Exhibit A is the empty tomb. Exhibit B is the numerous eyewitnesses.

Exhibit A:
The Empty Tomb

In Luke 24:1-3, we are told "on the first day of the week, very early in the morning... certain other women... came to the tomb, bringing the spices which they had prepared. But they found the stone rolled away from the tomb. They went in and did not find the body of the Lord Jesus."

Many famous graveyards around the world attract thousands of visitors each year: the Egyptian pyramids, Westminster Abbey in London, and Arlington National Cemetery in Washington D.C. These cemeteries are famous for what they contain. However, the most renowned tomb in the world, visited by the most people, is not famous for what it contains, but for what it does not contain. The Garden Tomb in Jerusalem receives more notoriety than any other because it's an empty tomb.

Yet people say, "How do we know the empty tomb proves that Christ is risen? Perhaps there's another explanation." Throughout the years, skeptics have offered a whole smorgasbord of fanciful, fictitious theories as to what happened to the body of Jesus. Yet, their theories have failed to dispel the Resurrection because none of them fit the facts.

For instance, the "wrong tomb" theory. Supposedly, the women went to the wrong tomb, saw the grave clothes but no body, and just assumed Jesus had risen from the dead. The skeptic points out, "Hey, women are sometimes flighty, quick to jump to conclusions. These girls just got carried away."

A few years ago, my wife Kathy and I visited Ft. Lauderdale where she grew up. She wanted to visit her father's grave, so we drove up to this huge graveyard with no gravestones, just markers. Though it had been years since she'd been there, she remembered the exact location of his gravesite.

Isn't it absolutely ludicrous and downright insulting to suggest that these women, who dearly loved Jesus, would forget the whereabouts of His grave? Not only would the women have to forget the tomb's location, but the disciples, the Jews, and the Romans would also have had to visit the wrong tomb to confirm their story. Do you really believe Joseph of Arimathea would have forgotten his own tomb?

Certainly once the disciples began to preach about the Resurrection—if they had gone to the wrong grave—the enemies of Christianity would have uncovered their mistake. The whole movement would have run amuk if someone had simply presented the body, but they couldn't, for Jesus was alive.

Next, there is the "swoon" theory. This theory purports that Jesus didn't really die; He just fainted and fell unconscious. The disciples only thought He was dead. They took Him off the cross and placed Him in a cool damp tomb. The chilly air eventually revived Him, but the disciples thought He had risen.

The Koran was an early perpetrator of this theory.

Others have suggested that Jesus had been drugged, appearing dead when He wasn't. Remember, the Romans offered Jesus a painkilling potion which He refused. Jesus said no to any form of sedative. His death was a deliberate effort to bear the full brunt of sin's punishment.

Those who doubt the reality of Christ's death need to take a closer look at what happened to Jesus in His final hours. Awake all night in the Garden, His sweat was like great drops of blood. He was tried six times, beaten, and a crown of thorns thrust into His scalp. He was too weak to carry the crossbar, which means before Jesus got to the cross, He had suffered tremendous blood loss. Then, on the cross, the soldiers perforated His hands and feet, and a spear pierced His side.

In the March 1986 issue of the prestigious Journal of the American Medical Society, an article was published entitled "On the Physical Death of Jesus Christ." Here's an excerpt...

> Clearly, the weight of historical and medical evidence indicates Jesus was dead before the wound to His side was inflicted and supports the traditional view that the spear, thrust between His right ribs, probably perforated

not only the right lung but also the pericardium and heart, and thereby ensured His death. Accordingly, interpretations based on the assumption that Jesus did not die on the cross appear to be at odds with modern medical knowledge.

Remember, too, Jewish burial required dressing a corpse with as much as a hundred pounds of spices, then wrapping it in tightly wound strips of cloth.

Now you tell me. How does a man suffer a severe loss of blood, the trauma of torture, a ruptured heart, and the suffocation of burial, only to wake up three days later, free himself, move a two-ton tombstone, fight a trained Roman sentry, and then be in the condition to impress His disciples? Believe that, and I've got some swampland I'd like to sell you. It takes more faith to believe Jesus didn't die—that it was all a hoax—than to believe the biblical account.

There is a third possible suggestion: the "legend" theory. This is the notion that the Resurrection was a legend that developed over time. The idea is that stories about Jesus passed from mouth to mouth, and as they did, they were embellished and stretched until they became mythological.

Of course, if this were true, the New Testament would need to be written years after the fact, perhaps the third or fourth century—late enough so that no one living during the Resurrection could refute its assertions. The New Testament though was written within thirty years of what it reports. Today, we have fragments of the New Testament dating back to 120 AD and quotations from even earlier.

The New Testament was written at a time when eyewitnesses were alive and could have either refuted or validated its claims. These eyewitnesses could even have been cross-examined. If an event like the Resurrection were not true, the New Testament would've been quickly shot down as myth.

Finally, some skeptics have suggested the "stolen body" theory. This is the granddaddy of all false theories. When news of the Resurrection first broke, this is the theory the Jews fostered to explain it away. Matthew 28:11-13 says, "Behold, some of the guard came into the city and reported to the chief priests all the things that had happened. When they had assembled with the elders and taken counsel, they gave a large sum of money to the soldiers, saying, "Tell them. His disciples came at night and stole Him away while we slept."

Of course, this theory was shot full of holes from the beginning. If the soldiers were asleep, how did they know it was the disciples who stole the body? Any lawyer would love to cross-examine that statement. And how did the disciples move a two-ton stone without waking the guard?

Besides, these soldiers were not about to fall asleep. Roman soldiers were killed for botching a job. These guys were warriors, killing machines. One of these soldiers would make John Wayne look like a sissy—and in an outfit dispatched to do guard duty there was usually, not one, but sixteen soldiers in the unit.

You tell me. Which one of our brave, fearless disciples is going to lead the charge against these sixteen armed Roman rambos? What about Peter? The night before the Crucifixion, he denied the Lord in front of a little girl. On the same night, all the disciples forsook Jesus. How were they going to muster enough courage to pull off a hijack? Besides, if they had succeeded, what would they have gained by such a hoax?

If preaching the Resurrection had made the disciples millionaires, or enabled them to draw huge fallowings, and garner appearances on the talk show circuit, maybe there'd be a motive. But these guys were beaten for preaching the message, and not once, but over and over and over. All eleven disciples who followed Jesus died in poverty and obscurity. Men will die and suffer for a lie if they believe it to be true, but no one in their right mind suffers for what they know is a hoax.

When we scrutinize the evidence, we realize only one person could have moved the stone, Jesus Christ Himself.

Exhibit B:
The Numerous Eyewitnesses

Not only does the empty tomb prove the Resurrection, but even more impressive were the multitude of eyewitnesses that saw the risen Christ. There were the women, Peter, the two men on the road to Emmaus, the disciples minus Thomas, then later the disciples plus Thomas, and seven disciples who ate breakfast with Jesus on the Sea of Galilee.

Paul adds in 1 Corinthians 15:6, "He was seen by over five hundred brethren at once, of whom the greater part remain to the present." In other words, most of the five hundred were still around. Paul is saying, "If you don't believe me, here are the phone numbers and addresses—look 'em up and talk to them personally.

Realize that if you brought a group of five hundred people into a courtroom and each person spent just ten minutes on the witness stand, their collective testimony would take about eighty-three hours. Just two or three corroborating witnesses can send a man to jail. The Resurrection's day in court would prove to be the most lopsided trial in history.

Notice, too, that none of the eyewitness reports were staged. In fact, the first person Jesus appeared to was Mary, a woman. This would never have happened if the disciples were fabricating a hoax. Women in Jewish culture were not considered reliable witnesses. They were thought to be too emotional. At first, even the disciples didn't believe Mary.

Nothing about any of the eyewitness reports smells of a conspiracy. Actually, the different reports are so diverse and random it would be impossible for the most skilled attorney to discredit the testimony.

There are several ways attorneys try to damage the testimony of an eyewitness. First, they try to prove the witness had a motive to lie. We've already seen this was not the case with the followers of Jesus. They were persecuted for what they preached. The Resurrection meant repression, not riches.

The second way to disprove the testimony of an eyewitness is to prove that what he or she saw was actually a hallucination—a vision, the creation of a vivid imagination. Jesus was careful to prove He was not a mere vision. He told Thomas to touch His scars. The women grabbed His feet and worshipped Him. Jesus even ate fish by the seashore. It was obvious to the disciples, over the forty days in which Jesus appeared to them, that the resurrected Christ was not a ghost or figment of imagination. Jesus possessed a real body.

Psychologists tell us there are certain conditions under which a hallucination is prone to occur, none of which were characteristic of the post-resurrection appearances of Jesus Christ.

First, for a person to hallucinate, they need to be prone to a vivid imagination, or an unstable emotional make-up. Perhaps you could claim this of the women, but what about the hardheaded fishermen who followed Jesus? Or the pragmatic tax-collector? Or the militarily savvy zealot?

Second, a hallucination is a subjective, individual experience. Therefore, it's unlikely that two people would ever have the same hallucination at one time.

This is why Paul said that five hundred people saw Jesus simultaneously.

Third, environmental conditions are a cause for hallucinations—dim lights, a relaxed mood, soothing sounds, etc. But Jesus appeared in a variety of situations: to the women in the morning, to the two men on the road to Emmaus in the afternoon, to the disciples at night. He appeared both indoors and outdoors, by a road, a lake, and in a house.

Fourth, a person who hallucinates usually repeats it sometime in his lifetime. The disciples' sightings of Jesus lasted forty days, then ceased.

Fifth, for a hallucination to occur there needs to be some kind of an anticipation or expectation. For example, take a woman who has endured the trauma of losing a son, yet she sits on her front porch in the afternoon and imagines him walking home from school. This is the type of person who is prone to hallucinate.

But the people who saw the risen Christ were shocked when they saw Him. Remember the mood of the eyewitnesses who saw Jesus? The women at the empty tomb were coming to anoint a dead body. At first, the disciples thought they'd seen a ghost. Thomas was skeptical when he was told the news. The doubtful disciple refused to believe in the Resurrection until he had actually seen Jesus for himself and touched the scars in His hands. Paul, too, was a hostile witness. Recall, he was headed to Damascus to kill Christians. He was certainly not expecting to meet the risen Christ.

If you were on trial and the prosecution began to put this kind of case together, you'd want to plea bargain. You'd realize you haven't got a chance. In fact, there is much more evidence we could consider.

Think of the circumstantial evidence that we could add to the empty tomb and eyewitnesses. Consider the change that took place among the disciples. How do you explain their transformation? Overnight, the disciples went from being wimps to witnesses. And what were they preaching? Their rallying cry was the Resurrection of Jesus Christ.

Think, too, of the birth of the Church. What provided the Jews the incentive to leave behind their Jewish moorings, forsake the Law, and trust in Christ? Nothing less than the Resurrection could have uprooted their tradition.

And what about the New Testament? It was based on the reality of the Resurrection. Do you really think that the world's all-time nonfiction bestseller could be based on an event that never really happened?

Why do we worship on Sunday? For 1400 years Jews worshipped God on Saturday. Why suddenly change from Saturday to Sunday? What would provoke such a shift other than the anniversary of a very special event?

Last, but certainly not least, look at the millions of changed lives down through the centuries. No one in the history of mankind has come close to influencing more people than Jesus Christ. It's certainly not the work of a dead man. Obviously from His activity Jesus is alive and well.

In the early 1920s, on the heels of the Bolshevik Revolution, a communist proponent was sent from Moscow to Kiev to lead an anti-God rally. For an hour, he abused the Christian faith. He mocked and ridiculed every truth that Christ died for and that Christians hold dear. When he was done, he opened the floor for questions. One Orthodox priest asked to speak. He turned to the crowd, and in his best liturgical fashion, he issued the ancient Easter greeting, "Christ is risen." The entire crowd rose to its feet and shouted the response,"He is risen indeed."

One fact stood in the way of the atheistic propaganda that day: the truth of the Resurrection. It's been said, "The Resurrection of Jesus stands fast as a fact, unaffected by the waves of skepticism that ceaselessly through the ages beat themselves against it."

The evidence is in, the verdict is certain, it can never be refuted, "Jesus Christ is risen." The Author of Christianity made a daring move. He placed all His eggs in one basket. He played "winner takes all" with the devil. God staked everything on one miraculous event. If Jesus failed, He'd be ignored and ridiculed and sail away into obscurity. But if He succeeded, He would win the right to be worshipped forever.

The empty tomb says to the philosopher, "Explain

this event, if you can"; to the scientist, "Repeat this event, if you can"; to the historian, "Refute this event, if you can"; to the skeptic, "Blot out this event, if you can"; and it says to us today, "Believe this event, if you will." Will you believe? Don't mess around with the One who holds the keys to life and death.

Saint Augustine wrote, "Jesus rose from the grave and departed from our sight that we might return to our heart, and there find Him. For He departed, and behold, He is here." Jesus came out of the empty tomb to live in your empty heart. To deny Him His place is to spurn the truth. It's to deny Him the spoils of His victory. Is it little wonder that the punishment for unbelief is so severe?

If God were to visit us, could you think of a more convincing way for Him to reveal His identity than to overcome death? Don't turn your back on Jesus and miss the obvious. Jesus has risen from the dead. Don't keep Him on the outside of your life looking in. Open your heart to Him today.

Next, take a look behind the scenes to discover how the combat that took place in the heavenly realm 2000 years ago plays a part in our lives today.

IT IS FINISHED
by Bill Stonebraker

Six agonizing hours after being nailed to the cross, Jesus cried with a loud voice, "It is finished." He then bowed His head and dismissed His spirit.

Only three words—It Is Finished—yet so powerful and authoritative that they literally shook the earth beneath the cross and changed the destiny of man.

Some would have you believe they were words of defeat spoken by one who was perishing... "I am finished." Not so! They were words of victory and completion.

How can the words of a dying man be so powerful? After all. He is dying. It doesn't make sense. People generally would rather be remembered for how they lived, not how they died.

Great people have died in the past, uttering words of desperation and terror. The Last Words of Saints and Sinners by Lockyer chronicles the dying words of kings, nobles, and other prominent people. Recorded is their final effort at clinging to life before going into the next life:

Phillip the Third, King of France cried, "What an account I shall have to give to God! How I should like to live otherwise than I have lived."

Queen Elizabeth of England wailed, "All my possessions for one moment of time."

The Duke of Buckingham said, "I sported with the holy name of heaven. Now I am haunted by remorse, and I fear forsaken by God."

Kay the infidel in despair shrieked, "Hell! Hell! Hell!"

Foreign Minister under Napoleon, Perigood-Talleyrand's dying words were, "I am suffering, Sire, the pangs of the damned."

It is a frightful thing to die without hope, unprepared to face the consequences of living a reckless life, sowing the wind and at last reaping the whirlwind. At the same time, it is a glorious thing to die in hope of eternal life—to trust the victory Christ won on the Cross when He said, "It is finished."

Alexander the Second triumphantly declared, "I am sweeping through the gates, washed in the blood of the Lamb."

Charlemagne announced, "Lord, into Thy hands

I commend my spirit."

What will your final words be when you go from this life into the next? Words of joy and triumph? Or words of regret and panic?

Jesus' final words from the cross describe three truths that affect our lives. We can identify them by the acrostic DIE:

D = Devil's reign is finished
I = Inferiority is finished
E = Exile is finished

The Devil's Reign Is Finished

The devil ended man's reign in the garden; Jesus ended the devil's reign on the cross. God gave man ownership of the earth (Genesis 1:28). By man's disobedience to God and obedience to Satan, he forfeited ownership to the devil. Satan held rulership up until Jesus proclaimed, "It is finished."

> When He had disarmed the rulers and authorities. He made a public display of them, having triumphed over them through Him (Jesus).
>
> —Colossians 2:15

When Christ cried, "It is finished," He disarmed

the devil. That is to say, Jesus took away his authority and power. Being disarmed literally gives the picture of "stripping off a garment and taking it away." The devil is stripped of power over the Christian's life. We might hear the devil roar. We may even feel him biting at our heels, but realize, he's a toothless wonder. The Lord pulled his fangs and rendered him powerless.

You might say, "Wait a minute. If the devil's reign of power is over, why does it appear that he still has free rule on earth? Look at all the evil in the world!"

You have put all things in subjection under His feet. For in subjecting all things to him. He left nothing that is not subject to him. But now we do not yet see all things subjected to him.

—Hebrews 2:8

On the cross, Jesus redeemed the world back to God. It's His, but He has not yet taken possession of it.

Imagine that you made a land deal. You buy the property while tenants are still living on it. When you choose to take possession of the real estate, you will have to notify the tenants that you will evict those that don't belong there. Likewise, Satan has usurped authority over what belongs to God. Jesus paid the price to redeem back the world and those in it. Soon He will come for what is rightfully His (Revelation 5) and evict Satan and those who reject His ownership.

God lives in the eternal now. He speaks of future events as if they have already taken place. We live in a time-space continuum. To us, these things are still in the future, but to Him it is finished.

For this reason, rejoice, O heavens and you who dwell in them. Woe to the earth and the sea, because the devil has come down to you, having great wrath, knowing that he has only a short time.

—*Revelation 12:12*

Notice, in this passage, the Lord says Satan has come down to Earth. The Lord uses the word woe as a warning of future events. If we think things are bad now, wait until Satan is cast to Earth; he will cause total havoc seeing he has a very short time.

And the devil who deceived them was thrown into the lake of fire and brimstone, where the beast and the false prophet are also; and they will be tormented day and night forever and ever.

—*Revelation 20:10*

The final demise of the devil is declared. He is disarmed presently, but in this passage God speaks of his ultimate destruction. Because He sees beyond here and now. God sees the devil as a defeated foe. We can't see the future. However, the time will come when Satan will be cast into the lake of fire, along with the false prophet and the beast, as well as death and Hades.

We also find, in this same chapter, that God is going to resurrect the unrighteous dead. They will face eternal punishment because their names are not written in the Book of Life. Maybe the terror of those who exit this life and see a glimpse of eternity apart from Christ is a wake up call to those who have put off accepting Jesus as Lord and Savior.

When we speak of Gehenna, outer darkness, or the lake of fire, it describes a place God never intended for man. It is a place prepared for the devil and fallen angels. If a man rejects Christ, God has no choice but to reject him and sentence him to eternal damnation. A person has to step over the body of Jesus to get into eternal torment. God has made it difficult for man to be damned. Those who refuse to repent will not have their names written in the Book of Life, and they will be thrown into the lake of fire that burns forever and ever.

The devil has basically been erased from the future. He has no part in God's future kingdom. Revelation 11:15 tells us, "The kingdom of the world has become the kingdom of our Lord and of His Christ; and He will reign forever and ever." The book of Revelation tells the future from God's point of view. The New Jerusalem is in place, and God declares, "I am the Alpha and the Omega, the Beginning and the End." To Him, it's a done deal.

Right now, we live in time present—we have yet to see the future, but we can read about it in the Bible. By faith we believe the devil's reign is finished. Soon we will visibly, physically see it to be true.

In the early 1800's, an artist, who was also a great chess player, painted a picture depicting a young man in a chess match with the devil. The youth moved the white pieces and the devil the black. At stake was eternal freedom if the young man won, or he'd become the devil's slave if he lost. The infidel artist pictured Satan as having moved his queen and announcing checkmate in just four moves. The young man's hand hovered over his rook, beads of sweat on his ashen face. There was no hope. The devil won. His soul was forfeited forever.

For many years the painting hung in a great art gallery in Cincinnati. Chess players from around the world came to view the picture. They agreed with the artist: the boy looses, the devil wins. One skeptic studied the painting and concluded that only one chess player on earth could give assurance that the artist was right in his conception of the winner. Paul Morphy of New Orleans was, in his day, the undefeated, supreme chess master. It was arranged for Morphy to come to Cincinnati to view the painting. As he stood concentrating before the picture for five—ten—twenty—thirty minutes, he lifted and lowered his hands, as in imagination. He made and eliminated moves. Suddenly he paused. His eyes burned with the vision of an unthought of combination. He shouted, "Young man. That's the move. That's the move." To everyone's amazement, the old master detected a combination that defeated the devil and proved the artist wrong.

You might have thought the same about your own life, "It's hopeless. The devil wins, I lose." Maybe you have been under his power for a long time. You feel like there is no way out: "checkmate in four moves." You think, "My life can't change. I've tried and nothing's happened." You assume "once a failure, always a failure." "I started out a loser, and I'll end up a loser." That is a lie and comes from the father of lies, Satan. The fact is, the devil's the loser. He was defeated at the cross. He is finished. The only move you need to make is toward Jesus Christ. Abide in Him and He will do the rest.

Inferiority Is Finished

"I" represents the inferior position Jesus took in becoming a man. The dictionary defines inferior as "lowly in rank; of less value; a position below others." The triumphant entry describes Him as "lowly and riding on a donkey." We see His humiliation through the eyes of Isaiah: He was despised and forsaken of men, a man of sorrows and acquainted with grief; and like one from whom men hide their face He was despised, and we did not esteem Him (Isaiah 53:3).

Dishonor, contempt, and humiliation marked the Lords life: "But I am a worm and not a man, a reproach of men and despised by the people" (Psalm 22:6).

How about you? Do you ever feel this way? Lonely? Misunderstood? When tough times come, do friends seem to disappear?

In one episode of the Oprah Winfrey show, people were featured who had fallen from prominent positions and were now living on the street. An architect, a model and others. Through progressive stages, they went from the pinnacle of success to the dregs of the earth. What was significant was that choice might not have been a factor in their fall. Noteworthy is the fact that during their calamity, friends didn't want to have anything to do with them. "You are sleeping where?" "You have no money?" "You are homeless?" "Well, I'll see you later." These stricken souls all gave a sobering warning: "any one person is only two paychecks away from being on the street." They cautioned that it could happen to anyone.

Jesus felt forsaken by all. In one breath the crowd cried, "Hosanna, Blessed is He who comes in the name of the Lord, King of Israel," and in the next, "Crucify Him." While on the cross, they mocked Him and taunted, "If you are the king of the Jews save yourself." He could have saved Himself, but if He would have. He could not save us.

Maybe you feel abandoned and forsaken. So did Jesus. He can identify with you and help. "For since He Himself was tempted in that which He has suffered, He is able to come to the aid of those who are tempted" (Hebrews 2:18).

Do you feel like you're going down for the last time? Is humiliation your constant companion? There are times when people can make us feel very small. We are relegated to an inferior position, as was Jesus. The good news about suffering and those who endure it is that good can come from it. James 5:10-11 tells us:

> As an example, brethren, of suffering and patience, take the prophets who spoke in the name of the Lord. We count those blessed who

endured. You have heard of the endurance of Job and have seen the outcome of the Lord's dealings, that the Lord is full of compassion and is merciful.

Those who have gone before us bring encouragement to us when it comes to suffering. Job is such a great example of one who lost it all yet never "took it out on the Lord," so to speak. Instead of blaming God, he blessed Him, saying, "Naked I came from my mother's womb, and naked I shall return there. The Lord gave and the Lord has taken away. Blessed be the name of the Lord" (Job 1:21).

We can sometimes feel less valuable than God has made us. We may experience feelings of inferiority. Remember Jesus willingly took an inferior position allowing Himself to be misunderstood with the view that victory was forthcoming. Fruit always follows suffering.

It has been said, "Success and suffering are vitally and naturally linked together. If you succeed without suffering, it is because someone else has suffered before you; if you suffer without succeeding, it is that someone else may succeed after you."

Consider Jesus at His most vulnerable time. When He was in greatest need, people let Him down.

In the garden of Gethsemane He expresses, "My soul is exceeding sorrowful to the point of death. Watch with me." He asked His closest friends to pray with Him during His hour of anguish; they failed Him and fell asleep. When He was arrested, they ran. Peter followed from afar and when pressed if he knew Jesus, he denied Him. Not once or twice but three times, and with an oath, "I do not know the man."

It is hard to imagine, but good came from the situation. Even though Jesus' trusted disciples abandoned Him, God did not. An angel was sent to minister to Him in the garden, like the Father did after the wilderness temptation when Jesus forced a showdown with the devil.

Although Peter ran and hid when the Lord needed him most, failure brought fruit in Peter's life. Eventually Peter recovered and learned a valuable lesson from his ordeal. In writing about suffering, Peter says, "For you have been called for this purpose, since Christ also suffered for you, leaving you an example for you to follow in His steps, who committed no sin, nor was any deceit found in His mouth; and while being reviled. He did not revile in return; while suffering. He uttered no threats, but kept entrusting Himself to Him who judges righteously (1 Peter 2:21-23).

Tradition says that Peter suffered through

martyrdom, saying, "I am not worthy to be crucified as my Lord. Crucify me upside down." Peter learned to take the inferior position as his Lord had. He also learned the valuable lesson of how God views those who do: "Therefore humble yourselves under the mighty hand of God, that He may exalt you at the proper time" (1 Peter 5:6).

In a true sense, inferiority is finished. Jesus Himself forever took the lowly position and exchanged our lowliness for His power.

> Have this attitude in yourselves which was also in Christ Jesus, who, although He existed in the form of God, did not regard equality with God a thing to be grasped, but emptied Himself, taking the form of a bond-servant, and being made in the likeness of men. Being found in appearance as a man. He humbled Himself by becoming obedient to the point of death, even death on a cross. For this reason also. God highly exalted Him, and bestowed on Him the name which is above every name.
>
> —Philippians 2:5-9

We now look forward to sharing in His glory and His kingdom. "Listen, my beloved brethren: did not God choose the poor of this world (to be) rich in faith and heirs of the kingdom which He promised to those who love Him?"(James 2:5). Truly inferiority is finished. Jesus said, "The glory which you have given me I have given to them, that they may be one, just as We are one" (John 17:22).

Exile Is Finished

We were once far off from God, or exiled, but now we are brought near to Him...

But now in Christ Jesus you who formerly were far off have been brought near by the blood of Christ (Ephesians 2:13).

God was in Christ reconciling the world to Himself, not counting their trespasses against them, and He has committed to us the word of reconciliation (2 Corinthians 5:19).

It is awesome to realize the alienation we once experienced is no longer permanent. God has brought us to Himself by the blood of His son Jesus Christ. And not only so, but we also joy in God through our Lord Jesus Christ, by whom we have now received the atonement (Romans 5:11).

The word atonement literally means "to be reconciled or brought back to God." We might interpret it as "at-one-ment." Jesus' sacrifice sets us into right relationship with God.

Only a perfect sacrifice could satisfy God. Jesus, God's only begotten son, is that perfect offering. We are not able to make our own sacrifice because we are not perfect or sinless. God provided a sacrifice on our behalf. "And although you were formerly alienated and hostile in mind, engaged in evil deeds, yet He has now reconciled you in His fleshly body through death, in order to present you before Him holy and blameless and beyond reproach" (Colossians 1:21-22).

Did you know there are over 1,300 references to atonement in the Bible? God desires that we know, beyond a shadow of a doubt, that we are saved and brought near to Him. Our exile is over—it is finished!

In 1944, toward the end of World War II, Shoichi Yokoi fled to a cave in Guam and hid out for years after the war ended. Fearing for his life, he only came out at night to forage for rats, frogs, snails, shrimp, nuts and mangos. He made clothing out of tree bark. He knew the war was over because of leaflets that had been dropped and scattered throughout the jungle, but he feared execution if he showed himself. Finally, 28 years later, two hunters discovered him and convinced him that it was safe, he no longer needed to hide. They took him by plane to his home and gave him new clothes and food. Best of all, he was given freedom.

Are you hiding from God? You don't have to hide anymore. The war is over, Jesus won your freedom. God offers His grace and love so you can enjoy a relationship with Him.

The Bible describes God's great love for us as being "beyond finding out." His forgiveness is pictured this way: "Purify me with hyssop, and I shall be clean; wash me, and I shall be whiter than snow" (Psalm 51: 7). We use the term white as snow to describe the ultimate whiteness. In this passage, the cleansing power of Christ's blood pronounces us "whiter than snow." When snow falls, it picks up trace elements of dirt from the atmosphere. But when Jesus cleanses a sinner, there are no lingering trace elements of sin and guilt. Snow pales in comparison to His whitening work in our lives. No sin is too great, no amount of evil has done too much that it can diminish the cleansing power of Christ's blood.

The devil may try to convince you he's made "checkmate in four moves," that whatever move you make he's won, but we need to keep in mind that his reign is finished. We now see the future through the eyes of Jesus from the Word of God: Jesus wins, Satan loses. He is cast into the lake of fire. We are reigning and ruling with Christ.

For now, the devil is up to no good. He seeks to

rob, steal, and destroy. Burdening and discouraging hearts, he fills lives with strife, pain and loneliness. He tempts us to sin; it takes a tremendous toll on us. Inferiority makes us feel less than what God has made us. Feelings of worthlessness becomes a heavy weight to bear. The good news is that Jesus took a lowly position, an inferior place, so that through His poverty we might become rich (2 Corinthians 8:9). His lowliness has become our honor. We have been made in the image of God; our true identity is in God alone. Jesus has conquered over the negative feelings we have about ourselves because of sin and the fall. Most importantly, we don't have to hide from God any longer.

If you are not sure about your salvation, there is only one move you need to make: toward God. He will give you the grace to make that move. The devil will try to block the effort, but if God be for you who can stand against you? "Greater is He that is in you, than He that is in the world" (1 John 4:4).

Anything that stands in your way—the devil, inferiority, exile—is finished.

Join Jon Courson as he examines the condition of man's heart and comforts us with the knowledge that our failures are met by the faithfulness of God...

What Does Easter Mean to You and Me?

THE HOPE OF EASTER
by Jon Courson

One would have thought the first Easter was a day filled with total exhilaration and unbridled joy. After all, the Promised One, the Redeemer, the Messiah had risen from the dead. But a closer look at the 24th chapter of Luke's Gospel tells us differently. Notice the words Luke employs to tell the story ...

> 4. And it came to pass, as they were much perplexed...
>
> 5. And as they were afraid. . .
>
> 11. And their words seemed to them as idle tales (literally, "babblings from a fevered mind"), and they believed them not...
>
> 12. Then arose Peter, and ran unto the sepulchre; and stooping down, he beheld the linen themselves, and departed, wondering in himself (literally, "deeply questioned") ...
>
> 37. But they were terrified and affrighted, and supposed that they had seen a spirit. . .
>
> 38. No wonder, then, that Jesus asked his fearful disciples, "Why are ye troubled? and why do thoughts arise in your hearts?"

I suggest the events of the previous night provide the answer to Jesus' question. After all, a mere three days earlier, not only were the dreams and hopes of the disciples buried in the Garden Tomb along with their Best Friend, but so was their failure, fickleness, and faithlessness towards Him.

You see, the night before Jesus was taken away, nailed to a cross and slaughtered for their sin, what were the disciples doing? They were arguing in the Upper Room about which of them was the greatest (Luke 22:24).

Then, after one of their own left to betray Him, Jesus told them they all would be offended with Him and scatter from Him.

"Not me!" declared Peter. "Even if everyone else leaves You, I won't. You can count on me"—a statement with which all of the disciples agreed (Matthew 26:33-35).

That same evening, Jesus asked the disciples to pray with Him in His time of agony. But what did they do?

They fell asleep.

When they awoke to the sight of a company of Roman soldiers advancing upon them, they ran for their lives. Thus, the night before Jesus' death—a night when they could have proven their loyalty and love for the One who so loved them—what did the disciples do?

They argued and boasted, fell asleep, and fled so far that all except one were nowhere to be seen at the foot of the Cross the next morning.

No wonder the disciples were afraid. The One who died for them knew how they had completely and utterly forsaken Him. And now He was back.

Perhaps you know just how they felt. Perhaps you're saying, "If Jesus came back today, I would be fearful as well because, just like the disciples, I have failed miserably. I gave my life to Him ten years ago—or five months ago—but since that time, I've denied that I've known Him, turned my back on Him, slept when I should have prayed, and fled when I should have followed. There's no way I could face Him now."

But guess what. His Word to you is the same as it was to those terrified disciples, and what a Word it is ...

Thus it is written, and thus it behooved Christ to suffer, and to rise from the dead the third day: And that repentance and remission of sins should be preached in His name among all nations, beginning at Jerusalem.

—Luke 24: 45-46

Did you catch that? To you who would feel "affrighted" and terrorized if Jesus came back today, to you who feel you're unworthy of His love, to you who have failed Him time and time again, Jesus says:

Your faithlessness is the very reason I died. I came that you might *repent*—that you might change the way you think, that you might no longer be afraid I am disappointed with you, or will give up on you. I came to *forgive* you.

Maybe, like the disciples, you find yourself thinking, "I've failed the Lord so badly that all I can do is run away and hide." But the fact that you are hearing His Word to you today shows that, just as He did to the disciples. He comes to you preaching "repentance and *remission* of sins."

This is the great news of Easter Sunday. I don't care what sin with which you've been involved, or what sin with which you presently struggle. The fact of the matter is: Your sin is *forgiven*. It's *gone*. All that remains for you to do is confess it instead of trying to deny it or run from it.

You have sinned. So have I. If you have opened your heart to Jesus, be assured that He died in your place, and in so doing purchased complete forgiveness of all of your sins—past, present, and future. That is how He can say to us, as He said to His disciples,

"Peace be unto you" (Luke 24:36).

And if you've never opened your heart to Jesus, this is the day to do so because there's no need to fear once you embrace God's gracious, glorious gift of salvation. Come to Him today. Say, "Lord, I need forgiveness, and embrace this day Your gift of salvation"—and then listen for His Word of peace in your heart.

Jesus is risen. He is risen indeed.

And I'm so glad.